Robert Burns:
Maker of Rhymes

Robert Burns: Maker of Rhymes

Elisabeth Jane McNair

Illustrated by Scoular Anderson

VIKING

VIKING

Published by the Penguin Group
Penguin Books Ltd, 27 Wrights Lane, London w8 5tz, England
Penguin Books USA Inc., 375 Hudson Street, New York, New York 10014, USA
Penguin Books Australia Ltd, Ringwood, Victoria, Australia
Penguin Books Canada Ltd, 10 Alcorn Avenue, Toronto, Ontario, Canada m4v 3b2
Penguin Books (NZ) Ltd, 182–190 Wairau Road, Auckland 10, New Zealand

Penguin Books Ltd, Registered Offices: Harmondsworth, Middlesex, England

First published 1996
1 3 5 7 9 10 8 6 4 2

Filmset in Linotron Bembo by
Rowland Phototypesetting Ltd, Bury St Edmunds, Suffolk

Made and printed in England by
Clays Ltd, St Ives plc

A CIP catalogue record for this book is available from the British Library

ISBN 0–670–86838–8

In gratitude to Clive, without whose patient encouragement and computer skills this book (and its author!) would not have survived, and to Brian and Sally, who accepted Robert into the family

CONTENTS

ACKNOWLEDGEMENTS

I am most grateful to Sheena Andrew of Ayr Library, who first suggested this book, and to all those whose support has made it possible, especially John Manson at Burns Cottage; David Smith of Irvine Burns Club; friends Irene and Roy Storie, Dorrith Sim, Christy Danielles and Tom Morrall; and lastly Donald McIver, who entrusted a total stranger with precious reference books.

I acknowledge with gratitude the fine illustrations of Scoular Anderson and the wise guidance of Emma Matthewson and her colleagues through the minefield of publishing.

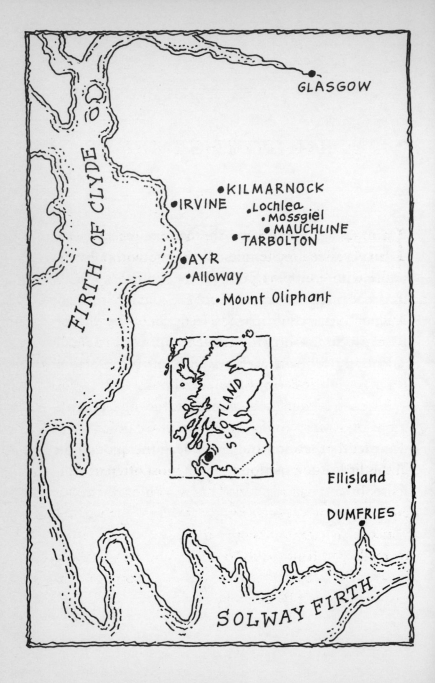

FIRTH OF CLYDE

GLASGOW

●KILMARNOCK
●IRVINE
●Lochlea
●Mossgiel
●MAUCHLINE
●TARBOLTON

●AYR
●Alloway

●Mount Oliphant

SCOTLAND

Ellisland

DUMFRIES

SOLWAY FIRTH

A NOTE TO THE READER

In 1754, a shy Highlandman became gardener on an Ayrshire estate. He fell in love with a lively redhead who, though full of common sense, couldn't write her name. Those two humble people, William and Agnes, were the parents of Robert Burns, whose poetry has enriched the whole world.

Robert was born at Alloway, near Ayr, on 25 January 1759 and died at Dumfries on 21 July 1796.

Because his poetry is mainly in Scots dialect, you may find some words you haven't heard before, but don't let that worry you. If you read the quotations in this little book out loud, you'll most often get the sense. In case you're puzzled, there's a glossary at the end of the book. A star by a word or phrase will let you know that it's explained there. As you continue to read, you'll probably find less and less need to look at the glossary and so will be encouraged to explore more of Robert's poetry.

Those of you who are Scots may recognize language that's still used today, especially in rural communities. Few words in standard English roll off the tongue like 'braw', 'bamboozle', 'glaikit', 'fash', 'jouk' or 'tapsalteerie'.*

You may enjoy finding more words and using them yourselves. In that way, you'll be helping to preserve a nation's heritage and the language used by its kings. This is what Robert wanted to do with his writing. For the hundreds of folk-songs he worked on in his later years, he refused any fee.

They were to be his gift to Scotland.

Chapter One

FIRST YEARS

Up in the morning's no' for me,
Up in the morning early.

A familiar feeling? But Robert Burns sang these lines over 200 years ago.

To make the most of daylight, his parents rose with the dawn, and, in a tiny house, there was no peace for sleepy-heads. At least getting up didn't take long, because no time was wasted on washing. Wouldn't you use water sparingly if you had to carry every drop from the well? In any case, people then didn't believe that cleanliness was important. Robert just kept on his warm night-clothes and added more layers by day. When he needed the toilet, he used a urine cask which was strangely referred to as 'the wash-tub'! The smells must have been quite powerful, and strongly scented plants like lavender were much needed.

Robert's first home was cosy, with its thick walls and small windows. His father, William, had seen to that when he built it himself from clay and stones. Imagine William's pride when he carried his laughing bride over the doorstep of their new home in Alloway. True, he had built only two rooms, one for the family and one for the animals, but they were his. Soon, though, he had a red face. Just ten days after Robert was born, part of the gable fell down. Agnes and her baby had to escape through the winter storm to a neighbour's house, leaving William to start the repairs.

You can visit the cottage at Alloway where Robert was born and imagine what family life would have been like in that little home. You can see, too, the box-bed – a hole in the wall measuring 1.75 metres long by 1.13 metres wide – where he was born.

Probably by the time Robert was walking, hard-working William had built on a new byre, leaving the original for extra working and sleeping space. As three more children were born, it was much needed. At first the babies slept in wooden cribs on the floor,  but then Robert and his younger brother Gilbert had to move into the half-loft over their parents' bed. Too bad if they wanted to get out during the night! Most of the time, it was warm to cuddle down together, listening to the wind howling in the lum⋆ and the rain spitting down on the warm hearth-stones. Warmth was also provided by the cows and pony champing on the other side of the dividing wall. And the lads were used to the scrabbling of rats in the thatched roof – too many for even the half-starved cats to cope with.

Robert wakened in the mornings to hear his mother singing as she sat on her four-legged stool to milk the cows, and he followed her as she worked around the steading. ★ As soon as he was old enough, he lent a hand – collecting the small white and brown fowls' eggs, skimming milk from the cream and cutting up curds to make soft white cheese. In the larder, he turned over the newly made cheeses every day so they would mature evenly. His help was needed, too, to turn the churn for butter-making and sometimes to pour brine into the pickling tub when a precious pig had been slaughtered and there was pork to be cured.

When the chapman's★ cart rumbled up to the door, Robert helped unload rolls of cloth for his mother's sewing. It was a red-letter day, too, when the packman called to empty from his bundle a treasure trove of needles, thread and thimbles, and also broadsheets with news and verse. In payment, these men would be given a supper of brose★ and lodging for the night.

Robert liked outdoor work best. When the byre had been 'muckit oot',★ he could get gloriously dirty, piling cow dung on to the 'midden'.★ This was just three paces from the door – a handy place to fling all the refuse, even dead dogs and cats. He could flap his arms wildly and shout to stop the hens and ducks eating the grain at threshing. Then, too, he had to keep the younger children away from the sharp 'heuk'★, used to cut corn, and also from the long-handled flail.★ This separated the grain from the stalk – a heavy job that the combine harvester does today. He enjoyed the warm lick of the cows'

tongues and the grateful nuzzling of the small, stocky pony as he fed it oats. Even helping to make the rough halter ropes from straw could be fun.

Like small boys the world over, Robert was a mischief, who sometimes hid from work. Can you blame him? Just like you, he needed time to throw 'chuckie stanes'⋆ and splash in puddles. Occasionally, he was allowed to play soldiers with Gilbert on the kitchen floor. Agnes kept an eye on them as she

cooked barley broth and cabbage in huge iron pots hanging from the 'swee'★ and browned oatcakes on the griddle over the fire. The vegetables she grew in her 'kailyard'★ weren't sprayed with insecticides and there were no crisps or Coke for treats. Yet, despite wholesome food, disease spread rapidly. It was a common occurrence for babies to die and young brides sewed 'mort sheets'★ with this in mind. Indeed, one friend of the Burns family could count only seven live children after sixteen births.

But Agnes was a careful mother and all her children lived to be grown up. She liked to see her family gathered by the 'ingle',★ with horn spoons and wooden drinking cups lifted down from the dresser and 'coggies'★ in laps. Later, Robert remembered those happy times when he described a decent, hard-working family like his own:

From scenes like these, old Scotia's★ grandeur
    springs
That makes her lov'd at home, rever'd abroad,
                'The Cotter's Saturday Night'

In the long winter evenings, Robert liked the soothing thrum of the spinning wheel as Agnes made yarn from sheep's wool. Since there weren't high-street shops, his clothes were all home-made.

Those for Sunday best were stored in the 'kist',★ with drab calf-length breeches and loose jackets kept for everyday. Children went barefoot because making shoes for quickly growing feet was considered an unnecessary expense. Even their mothers wore shoes only to church or to market. Some of these would be made by the souter,★ but there were also home-made 'straight shoes', which fitted either foot and were tied with tape in place of buckles. Shoe polish was unknown, but Robert blacked the kirk shoes with spit and soot scraped from the bottom of a pot.

At night, sweet-smelling smoke from the peat fire mingled with fumes from the oil lamps and tallow candles. In a contented haze, Robert listened to tales of ghosts, devils and witches told by his mother and old Betty Davidson, a relative who often stayed with the family and helped in the house. He sometimes clambered on to her lap, teasing by pulling her 'mutch'★ over her ears and tweaking the 'plaidie'★ round her shoulders. Stern, religious William Burns must have raised his eyebrows at some of the stories as he fetched the family Bible for evening prayers, but Betty's tales stayed in Robert's mind and many years later sparked off the ghostly tale of 'Tam o' Shanter'.

Chapter Two

SCHOOLING

When Robert was seven, his family moved two miles away to a seventy-acre farm at Mount Oliphant, overlooking the beautiful Firth of Clyde. A year earlier William and four friends had engaged a nineteen-year-old master called John Murdoch to teach their lads. Now Robert and Gilbert had to trudge further from the lonely hill-farm to the cold little schoolroom at Alloway. Often, John would come home with them, since he lived free in each of his pupils' homes – a good thing, too, because he earned only two and a half pence for each day's work. That would be about five pounds today.

When they lived at Alloway, a 'chaff'* had been pulled from under the box-bed and John slept on it at the fireside. Although Mount Oliphant was just a but and ben,* it had a steeply pitched roof and beneath this John shared the windowless attic with Robert and his three brothers.

John Murdoch delivered many a 'skelp',★ but he was a fine teacher and Robert soon learned to read. It can't have been easy, because the few books the master could get hold of were in English, not the Scots language Robert was used to. At first, he found his horn book helped him. This was a sheet of paper which had the alphabet, some numbers and spelling words and the Lord's Prayer written on it. Grubby hands couldn't spoil it since it was protected by a thin covering of transparent horn. The English

Robert absorbed in those days helped him later to write both fluently and correctly – amazing, because he had full-time education only until he was nine.

Sadly, John Murdoch decided to leave Alloway, so Robert's schooling stopped, apart from candlelit lessons with his father on winter evenings. Have you ever tried reading by candlelight? And can you imagine the effort of concentrating after a hard day's work in the fields? But William was well educated himself, for a farmer of the time, and he was keen for the boys to learn. (Girls were less important!) He spared his eldest son for two brief periods to attend local schools and then, when Robert was fourteen, sent him to Murdoch, who was now teaching at the Ayr grammar school. For three weeks Robert shared his schoolmaster's room, and it must have been a happy reunion.

Later, Robert was to meet with a less conscientious 'dominie'★ who fell asleep over his drink. Poking gentle fun at him, he wrote:

> Here lies Willie Michie's banes;★
> O Satan, when you tak' him,
> Gi'e him the schulin' o' your weans★
> For clever de'ils he'll mak' 'em.
> *'Epitaph for Willie Michie'*

The man's Christian name was really Ebenezer, but Robert found 'Willie' better suited to his rhyme!

With Murdoch's help in those three short weeks, Robert learned to read any book in French and some Latin too. Could you do that? A whole new world opened to the shabby lad when better-off boys lent him books to read that he would never have seen otherwise. Even at mealtimes now, he could be found sitting with his spoon in one hand and a book in the other.

Chapter Three

FARM LABOURER

Robert's father was no longer young or fit and he was only scraping a living from the poor soil. The land badly needed draining – essential in a climate as wet as Scotland's – but if he drained or improved the land, the rent was increased. Do you think that was fair? He badly needed his sons' help on the farm, for there were now seven children to feed on little money. 'We lived very sparingly,' Gilbert recalled. 'For several years butcher's meat was a stranger in the house.' Money must have been short indeed when William couldn't afford five pounds a year for hired help.

So Robert became principal labourer at Mount Oliphant. Dressed in his broad blue bonnet, a mud-spattered coat and corduroy breeks* with woollen leggings, he had to face the weather in all its moods. A black and white checked plaidie slung round his shoulders kept out some of the winter cold and was also useful if a sick lamb needed shelter. His wicker basket to carry manure was a dead weight on his shoulders. The plough he used had a heavy wooden frame and, although pulled by four horses, had to be carefully steered – hard work, since it bounced off the stony soil. Overworked and undernourished, the growing lad was already showing signs of the heart disease that eventually killed him.

Describing his brother's physical condition, Gilbert wrote, 'At this time, he was almost constantly afflicted in the evenings with a dull headache.' Later, Robert kept a bucket of water at his bedside into which he stuck his head when relief was needed!

'Hairst', or harvest, was the climax of a whole year's effort; the proceeds provided the food supply and paid the rent. It was common then to pair two young people to tie the crop into bundles and stack it by hand. At fifteen, Robert was put to work with a pretty girl called Nelly Kilpatrick and later remembered wondering 'why my pulse beat such a furious rataan when I looked and fingered over her hand to pick out the nettle-stings and thistles'. She had a sweet voice and so inspired Robert to write words for one of her favourite tunes — his very first song. Nelly especially liked the lines:

> She dresses ay sae clean and neat,
>   Both decent and genteel;
> And then there's something in her gait
>   Gars★ onie dress look weel.★
> > > > *'Handsome Nell'*

Robert must have been happy just to find a companion. For about six years, he had scarcely seen anyone but members of his own family, existing in what Gilbert called 'cheerless gloom' and working like a 'galley-slave'.

Chapter Four

EXPANDING HORIZONS

J ust in time to avoid total ruin, William escaped
from the tenancy of Mount Oliphant and, when
Robert was eighteen, the family moved to
Lochlea. Their farmhouse (now greatly altered)
nestled in a hollow near its marsh-ringed loch. It was
set in 130 acres, midway between Mauchline and
Tarbolton – a whole new area to explore. 'For four
years we lived very comfortably here,' wrote
Robert.

With six friends, he started the Bachelors' Club at Tarbolton where young men met to debate. Although still tired and starting to have attacks of depression, he found more time to think. He was forming a dislike of people who pretended to know everything and later wrote about them:

> A set o' dull conceited hashes★
>   Confuse their brains in college-classes
> They gang in stirks★
>   And come out asses.
> *'Epistle to J. Lapraik'*

In his own pocket, Robert always carried a book, but he felt that some people kept these just for show. He made fun of them by imagining worms eating their books:

> Through and through th' inspired leaves,
>   Ye maggots make your windings.
> But O respect his lordship's taste,
>   And spare the golden bindings.
> *'The Book-Worms'*

Feeling that his life lacked purpose, he decided he must do something to change it. The wonder crop of the time was flax, which was well suited to the clay soil and wet winds at Lochlea. Robert decided to learn the difficult process of 'dressing' the flax, making it ready for the womenfolk to spin into yarn. To do this, he had to move to the town of Irvine, ten miles away.

If proof were needed of his ability to work hard, the six months he spent labouring in the Irvine heckler's★ shop is enough. As he stooped to enter the mean two-roomed shack, he must have been choked by the heavy smell of grease and the oily dust that hung thick in the air. Robert worked at least ten hours a day and, for a time, slept on the filthy premises with work-horses for company. And he was actually paying for the experience. What a change of environment for someone used to clean farm air! No wonder concern for his son's health brought William to Irvine. Robert must have been ill indeed, for the local doctor visited him five times in the space of eight days.

Fortunately perhaps for the poet, a fire during hogmanay celebrations brought his tuition (and his money!) to an end. Nevertheless, he stayed on at Irvine for a further three months. Always interested in people, he became a close friend of sea captain Richard Brown, who made the momentous suggestion that Robert should publish his poems. A rare treat, too, was Templeton's bookshop, where he spent many happy hours reading ballads, the pop songs of his day.

From Irvine, he wrote his only letter to his father. It began: 'Honoured Sir'. How would your dad react if you called him that today? But Robert could defy his father, too. Much against William's wishes, he had made time to attend a dancing class, hopefully removing his farm boots first! William was not amused and Robert wrote, 'From that instance of rebellion he took a dislike to me.' Later, William lay dying and rambling on about his worries for one of his children. 'Is it me you mean?' asked Robert, coming to the bedside and trying to hide his tears.

After William's death, Robert and Gilbert moved the family to the 118-acre farm at Mossgiel, three miles away. Again, the farmhouse had two apartments, with a floored loft which sported three tiny rooms, and the one Robert shared with Gilbert had a skylight window. Riches indeed! Beneath this window sat a small table whose drawer held Robert's writing materials, and here he produced a steadily growing mountain of poetry.

But, as head of the family now, he was also full of good resolutions. 'I read farming books; I calculated crops; I attended markets,' he wrote. He was trying to keep abreast of the many improvements gradually taking place in the fields. Formerly, the ground had been ploughed into 'rigs'* whose width was only as far as a man's hand could scatter seeds. With

land now being enclosed, it was possible to grow crops in rotation, thus allowing one field to rest fallow each season. However, two years of bad seed and late harvests combined to discourage him. Literature and the lasses were becoming more interesting and he transferred his share of the farm to Gilbert.

Chapter Five

THE LASSES

Some of William's fears had been justified. At the age of twenty-five, Robert's dark good looks, tall, strong physique and glowing eyes were appealing. A brilliant talker, it was just a pity he had a biting tongue, but he'd inherited Agnes's charm and could bewitch any girl he wanted. And he wanted many! Soon the family's recent home help, Elizabeth Paton, presented him with an illegitimate daughter.

Robert hoped that baby Bess would inherit

> thy poor, worthless daddie's spirit,
>   Without his failins.
> *'A Poet's Welcome to His Love-Begotten Daughter'*

Calling her 'dear-bought Bess', he paid the fine imposed by the church for his conduct and passed her over to Agnes for safe keeping. Twins were his next offering to his long-suffering mother. They'd been born to Jean Armour, the bonny nineteen-year-old daughter of a Mauchline builder. Of course, he praised her in rhyme:

> Miss Miller is fine, Miss Markland's divine,
> Miss Smith she has wit, and Miss Betty is
>   braw★
> There's beauty and fortune to get wi' Miss
>   Morton;
> But Armour's the jewel for me o' them a'.
>   *'The Belles of Mauchline'*

Jean had heard him lament that he couldn't get a girl to love him as faithfully as his dog. Meeting him later, she asked if he'd found his lass yet. As she recounted it, Robert was walking where she was spreading her washing on the grass, to bleach in the sun. His little dog ran on to the clothes and she scolded him. Looking at Robert, Jean thought, 'I wadna think much o' you.' But she must have

changed her mind! When her highly respectable father heard of her pregnancy and saw their written promise of marriage, he fainted. His unfortunate daughter was hurriedly dispatched to stay with relatives in Paisley and Robert probably had a twinkle in his eye when he later rewrote the words of an old song:

O, whistle and I'll come to ye, my lad! . . .
    Tho' father and mother and a' should gae mad.
                'Whistle and I'll Come to Ye, My Lad'

Meanwhile, he was in love again – this time with Margaret Campbell, nursemaid in the home of his landlord, Gavin Hamilton. Because she spoke Gaelic, Robert called her 'Highland Mary'. 'My Highland lassie was a warm-hearted charming creature as ever blessed a man with generous love,' he wrote. As a token of faithfulness, the two exchanged Bibles while standing on opposite banks of the Faile stream. Mary's gift to Robert has never been found; the two-volume Bible he gave to her is in the cottage museum.

Sadly, Mary died soon afterwards and, three years later, Robert was still grieving:

O Mary dear departed shade!★
   Where is thy place of blissful rest?
See'st thou thy lover lowly laid?
   Hear'st thou the groans that rend his breast?

'Thou Lingering Star'

In 1920, Mary's 'place of blissful rest' was invaded when her grave was opened and part of a baby's coffin was found inside. Was Robert the father and did she die in childbirth? No one knows.

With both Armour and Campbell parents after him, Robert considered sailing off to Jamaica, but, changing plans, he eventually had his marriage to

Jean recognized in the eyes of the kirk. By that time, he had fathered her second set of twins. In all, she was to bear him nine children, four of whom lie buried in a sad little grave in Mauchline churchyard. How Jean must have wept! Though not as clever or as well educated as Robert, she was a loving wife and mother – certainly the faithful lass he had been looking for. She deserves to be honoured with a memorial but has none, while statues of 'Highland Mary' are to be found in Dunoon, Liverpool and New York.

It was Jean, after all, who patiently put up with Robert's continuing affairs of the heart. Without them, he wouldn't have produced the warmest and most tender love-songs that any poet has given the world.

In one of his most famous works, Robert rewrote an old ballad very beautifully:

> O, my Luve is like a red, red rose,
>   That's newly sprung in June.
> O, my Luve is like the melodie,
>   That's sweetly played in tune.

He was promising the lady of the moment:

> And I will luve thee still, my dear,
>   Till a' the seas gang dry.
>   *'My Luve is Like a Red, Red Rose'*

No doubt he believed it – at the moment!

Another well-known song is his lament for a lost love:

> Ye banks and braes o' bonnie Doon,
>   How can ye bloom sae fresh and fair?
> How can ye chant, ye little birds,
>   And I sae weary, fu' o' care!

Thou'll break my heart, thou warbling bird,
   That wantons★ thro' the flowering thorn
Thou minds me o' departed joys,
   Departed never to return.
                              'The Banks o' Doon'

But Robert was never sad for long and he enjoyed
making fun of the lasses too:

   Sic★ a wife as Willie had
      I wadna gi'e a button for her.
                              'Willie Wastle'

Chapter Six

TAM O' SHANTER

In what he considered his greatest poem, Robert painted a picture of a very cross lady. Her husband, Tam, had been to market in Ayr and had, as usual, drunk too much. He was riding home to his wife, the

> . . . sulky, sullen dame,
>   Gathering her brows like gathering storm,
> Nursing her wrath to keep it warm.

On his grey mare, Maggie,

> Tam skelpit on thro' dub and mire★
>   Despising wind, and rain, and fire.

But, at Alloway Kirk, he stumbled upon a riotous dance of witches and warlocks. Admiringly, he

cried, 'Weel done, cutty sark!'★ and in an instant the hags were after him.

> So Maggie runs, the witches follow,
> Wi' monie an eldritch skreich and hollow★

Knowing that witches couldn't cross a running stream, the farmer was making for the River Doon, and he was just in time. When a witch sprang at him, only the horse's tail remained on her side of the stream. So:

> the carlin★ claught★ her by the rump,
> And left poor Maggie scarce a stump.

The poor tailless horse served as a warning to travellers who might drink too much.

Tam's character was based on Douglas Graham of Shanter Farm, whose wife, Helen, was a scold, and the poet's tongue was firmly in his cheek when he commented:

> Ah, gentle dames, it gars me greet,★
> To think how monie counsels sweet,
> How monie lengthen'd, sage advices
> The husband frae the wife despises!
> *Tam o' Shanter*

No wonder Jean found Robert with tears of laughter running down his cheeks as he composed this masterpiece. It has fired imaginations worldwide and people come from far afield to see 'the auld, haunted kirk', 'Brig o' Doon' and 'Tam o' Shanter Inn', where the hero spent his merry evening. Even today, the broad cloth cap in which he is pictured is called a 'tam-o'-shanter' or 'tammy'.

Chapter Seven

THE BURNS SUPPER

An annual reminder of Robert is the Burns Supper. Five years after his death, nine Ayrshire gentlemen met together to eat sheep's head and haggis. Someone recited the 'Address to a Haggis'; toasts were drunk and it was agreed to meet again the following January. Thus started the practice of Burns Suppers, countless thousands of which now take place all over the world.

After the company has been seated, an old version of a grace Robert used is recited:

> Some ha'e meat and canna eat,
> And some wad eat that want it★
> But we ha'e meat and we can eat,
> And sae the Lord be thankit.
>   *'Selkirk Grace'*

Cockie-leekie* soup is usually first on the menu, after which the master of ceremonies asks everyone to stand for the arrival of the haggis. A kilted piper is first in the procession, followed by the chef with the haggis and a third person bearing two bottles of whisky. A slow handclap accompanies their progress to the top table. Then the haggis is praised in Robert's hearty words:

> Fair fa' your honest sonsie* face
> Great chieftain o' the puddin'-race!
> *'Address to a Haggis'*

As the line 'An' cut you up wi' ready slight'★ is reached, a knife is plunged into the 'warm, reekin', rich' food. The piper and chef next enjoy a dram★ of whisky before everyone drinks the first toast of the evening: 'To the Haggis'.

Not everyone thanks the Lord for haggis. It's made of lamb's heart, lungs and liver, all mixed

together with oatmeal and seasonings, and is tra-
ditionally sewn up in a sheep's stomach. Calculated
to make your mouth water? But, made by a good
butcher and mashed up with 'tatties and neeps',★ it
can taste warm and comforting in winter.

Dessert is often 'Scotch trifle' and after dinner the
speeches begin, the major one being the toast 'To the
Immortal Memory of Robert Burns'. For about half
an hour, the speaker encourages listeners to appreci-
ate Robert's life and achievements. This is followed
by two light-hearted speeches in which men and
women poke gentle fun at each other. When the men
have drunk their 'Toast to the Lasses', the ladies get
their chance to reply. Naturally they point out their
superiority, quoting Robert for support:

> Auld Nature swears the lovely dears
> Her noblest work she classes, O:
> Her prentice★ han' she try'd on man,
> And then she made the lasses, O.
> *'Green Grow the Rashes O'*

These are the main speeches but others may be
added. All are mingled with much-loved poetry and
song and the evening ends with 'Auld Lang Syne'.

Chapter Eight

FAIRS AND THE FUTURE

While living at Mossgiel, Robert enjoyed the social life of Mauchline, which was then a village of about 1,000 inhabitants. There, the poet found many people to observe and what better place to do so than at fairs? These combined welcome relief from a hard winter's grind with an opportunity to find partners amid the rollicking crowds. Travelling merchants sold wool, flax and yarn, hardware and crafts. Beggars produced gingerbread, fruit and candy out of filthy wallets to tempt 'bawbees'* from eager children. Punch and Judy provided new and fascinating entertainment alongside old favourites like spinning the top, hoop-rolling, kite-flying and skipping. Cockfighting was a gruesome spectacle which didn't appeal to Robert, but he gladly joined in dance and revelry lasting well into the night.

To the embarrassment of the clergy, there were

even wilder goings-on during the annual Holy Fair. The celebration started in seemly fashion, with a preacher addressing the crowd from an outdoor pulpit while they waited to receive communion in church. But, the minute the sacrament had

been administered, kirk boots were kicked off and the fun began. Games of chance were played on the cemetery gravestones and lads set out to impress lasses with feats of agility in the churchyard. As the

preacher called down both blessing and hellfire on all, Robert imagined the mixed feelings of the revellers:

> Here some are thinkin' on their sins,
>   And some upo' their claes;*
> Ane curses feet that fyl'd* his shins,
>   Another sighs and prays.
> > *'The Holy Fair'*

A modern version of the Holy Fair, held each year in Ayr, is fortunately a more dignified occasion, devoted to raising money for charity.

The pagan festival of Hallowe'en, still celebrated on 31 October, also fascinated Robert. Betty Davidson had told of the devilish spirits that reigned then and the many spells used to foretell the future, when

> . . . monie lads' and lasses' fates
> Are there that night decided.
> > *'Hallowe'en'*

Many folk customs were associated with this festival. In one, a lad and lass laid nuts on a bonfire and eagerly watched how they burned. If the nuts stuck together, their future happiness was assured, but if they sprang away, the couple would part.

Another custom was to hold a candle and eat an apple while combing the hair and looking in a mirror. Just try it! If you can do all that at once, you'll see in the glass the face of your future husband or wife – and you'll deserve to.

Robert had a go at fortune-telling himself when a new bridge was being built, against some people's advice. In 'The Brigs of Ayr', he made the thirteenth-century footbridge assure the new one jealously, 'I'll be a bridge when ye're a shapeless cairn!' Later, the new bridge was almost entirely washed away during a storm – and the old one still proudly spans the river today.

Chapter Nine

CHURCHGOING

Robert's poetry has made the people who lived over 200 years ago real. Though well intentioned, some of the churchmen were narrow-minded and self-important. When a Mauchline farmer and church elder, William Fisher, persecuted lawyer Gavin Hamilton for gathering potatoes on the Sabbath, Robert pictured Willie thanking God that he himself was

> . . . a pillar o' thy temple,
>   Strong as a rock –
> A burning and a shining light
>   To a' this place.
>   *'Holy Willie's Prayer'*

Some years later, Willie's light went out when he drank too much and froze to death in a snowy ditch!

It's hardly surprising that Robert had no time for the rigidly righteous, or 'unco guid', as he called them.

Although he couldn't believe, as many did, that God chose certain people to be favoured, he occasionally attended church. In some parishes, this was an entertainment in itself. People stood gossiping in the churchyard until the minister entered his pulpit, at which point they rushed inside, perched on their 'creepie'* stools and continued communicating by gestures even during the preaching. Dogs, cats, hens and chickens wandered in through the open doorway. A dog fight might result, with the owners coming to blows in the church. Finally, the minister's solemn act of blessing was largely ignored as

the congregation gathered its belongings ready for a speedy exit.

During one service, Robert was delighted to spy a louse creeping over the tall hat of a very smart lady. Laughing, he addressed the insect:

Now haud★ you there! ye're out o' sight,
  Below the fatt'rils,★ snug an' tight,
Na, faith ye yet, ye'll no be right,
  Till ye've got on it –
The vera tapmost,★ tow'rin' height
  O Miss's bonnet.

And he ended the poem with some wise words which are often repeated:

> O wad some Power the giftie gie us
> To see oursels as ithers see us
> *'To a Louse'*

About another church visit, the poet wrote:

> As cauld★ a wind as ever blew
> A caulder kirk and in't but few
> As cauld a minister's ever spak –
> Ye'se a' be het★ ere I come back.
> *'The Kirk at Lamington'*

This time, he hadn't been amused!

Chapter Ten

FAME

Now that Robert was composing such an amazing amount of poetry, he remembered his friend Richard Brown's advice to have it published. How proud the Burns family must have been when over 600 copies of his first collection, the now priceless Kilmarnock Edition, sold out within a month. With poems like 'The Cotter's Saturday Night', praising the good home-life of ordinary folk, no wonder it was popular! It cost only three shillings (fifteen pence) but was a work of art, with its carefully hand-cut and stitched pages within handsome blue covers. The book established Robert's reputation: at twenty-eight he was famous, although far from rich.

Of all the admirers he gained, Mrs Frances Dunlop was to become the most important to him. Nearly thirty years his senior, she could quite safely assume the role of mother-adviser. She gave Robert and Jean a splendid four-poster bed and exchanged a flood of letters with the young man. These, among 500 other letters written to friends, have survived and provide a valuable insight into the poet's thoughts and feelings.

There was something else that Robert liked about Mrs Dunlop. She believed herself descended from Sir William Wallace, who had long been his hero. One of the first books he'd read had been *The History of Sir William Wallace* and he'd thrilled to the brave soldier's exploits against the English king Edward I, hated 'Hammer of the Scots'. Robert shared William's love of Scotland and included him in his famous patriotic song:

> Scots, wha hae wi' Wallace bled,
>   Scots, wham Bruce has aften led,
> Welcome to your gory bed,
>   Or to victorie!
>
>   *'Scots, Wha Hae'*

The Kilmarnock Edition was so successful that Robert was advised to arrange publication of a second collection. So he exchanged his coarse home-spuns for an elegant blue coat with cream and blue lapels and set off for Edinburgh. Here was no un-educated 'ploughman poet'. Only his riding boots marked him as a country farmer and he spoke English better than many he met. True, his accom-modation was humble: half the bed of a young friend, John Richmond, in the Lawnmarket. But he was meeting the gentry!

Noble homes were thrown open to him and he set off on tours of the Borders, the Highlands and Stirlingshire – even rising to the dizzy heights of a post-chaise, or horse-drawn carriage.

When his second collection (not surprisingly called the Edinburgh Edition) appeared at the same time in both London and America, Robert was a poet of the world. But success didn't spoil him. Although he could adapt to all sorts and conditions of people, he was perhaps least at home with the gentry. He was to become genuinely fond of the Earl of Glencairn, but, when he'd gone to the considerable expense of finding a grey long-tailed coat and black gloves for the occasion, he wasn't invited to the Earl's funeral.

At an Edinburgh tea party, Robert had met Mrs Agnes McLehose, a married woman about his own age whose husband had deserted her. In over eighty letters they exchanged, they used nicknames to avoid the attention of Edinburgh gossips. Robert took 'Sylvander', meaning 'man of the woods', from the name of a popular romantic hero, and

Agnes chose 'Clarinda', from Spenser's poem 'The Faerie Queene'. When they parted, Robert wrote a song with some of the saddest words ever composed:

Had we never lov'd sae kindly,
    Had we never lov'd sae blindly,
Never met – or never parted –
    We had ne'er been broken-hearted.
                                    'Ae Fond Kiss'

Back with Jean, Robert moved to a 170-acre farm at Ellisland, about six miles north of Dumfries. There, he was able to have a five-roomed farmhouse built for his family, and Jean became the proud owner of the very latest iron cooking stove. It still works today! While Robert laboured outdoors, Jean made butter and cheese in the separate 'milk-hoose' and smoked her hams on meat-hooks hanging from the kitchen ceiling.

Gradually, standards of living had been improving. The tedious task of cutting and drying peat was less necessary now that coal was readily available. And Jean could cook a greater variety of food. When Robert was born, potatoes were hardly known as a crop, but now they provided a tasty and nourishing addition to the diet. Jean served beef and mutton boiled in vegetable broth and shared with neighbours a huge brass pan for making jams and jellies from gooseberries and wild blackberries. The 'guid-wives'★ had discovered that jam was a remedy for coughs, and jelly an excellent medicine for sore throats. Toothache, from which Robert suffered increasingly, was another matter, for there was no effective relief.

There was a stone-walled kitchen garden, at the end of which was the 'privy'★ – indoor toilets being restricted to the rich. Beyond the house were the byre and stabling with the stone dykes which Robert built to fence in his cows. He must have built well, for they still stand today. Although single-storey, the farmhouse had a loft space with attic rooms where two female domestics and two male farm servants slept. Lucky people they were, too, for they ate in the house (although separately from the family). They earned four shillings (twenty pence) a week as well as such clothes as were needed – and had time off to attend communion!

Chapter Eleven

THE SEEING EYE

Pet sheep were regular invaders of the house at Ellisland, for Robert cared about animals – and plants, too. To you and me, a daisy may be just a pretty weed. To the poet, it was a 'Wee modest, crimson-tipped flow'r'.

To the 'bonnie gem' adorning his field, he wrote:

> There, in thy scanty mantle* clad,
>   Thy snawie bosom sun-ward spread,
> Thou lifts thy unassuming head
>   In humble guise.
>
> 'To a Mountain Daisy'

With fond memories of the family pet, killed on the night before his father's death, he imagined that two dogs had souls and could speak with human voices. In this fable, Caesar (the rich man's dog) saw how the poor were treated and thought they must be miserable. But, speaking through Luath (the poor man's dog), Robert pointed out that there are many

kinds of happiness which money can't buy. He added a very true comment on human nature:

But human bodies are sic★ fools,
   For a' their colleges and schools,
That when nae real ills perplex them,
   They make enow★ themselves to vex them.

'The Twa Dogs'

Another famous poem shows his compassion for animals. Disturbing a mouse with his plough, he sympathized:

> Wee, sleekit,★ cow'rin, tim'rous beastie,
>   O what a panic's in thy breastie!

He was sorry to have spoiled its 'wee-bit housie', reflecting sadly:

> The best-laid schemes o' mice an' men
>   Gang aft agley.★
>   *'To a Mouse'*

Of all his quotations, this is one of the most popular, and perhaps Robert was thinking of himself when he wrote it.

Chapter Twelve

GENTLEMAN OF THE EXCISE

Ellisland proved a bad bargain and had to be sold. Robert was often ill with headaches, fever and depression, and was trying to do two jobs at once. Knowing only too well the risks in improving a run-down farm, he had also applied for a job as a tax collector, making sure duty was paid on goods coming into the Dumfries area. Naturally, the exciseman, as he was called, wasn't popular, and he made fun of himself, suggesting:

> The De'il's awa, the De'il's awa,
>   The De'il's awa wi' the Exciseman!
> He's danc'd awa, he's danc'd awa,
>   He's danc'd awa wi' the Exciseman!
>   *'The De'il's Awa wi' the Exciseman'*

The nearby coast was a favourite haunt for smugglers bringing in brandy, silk and tobacco from less highly taxed Continental ports. With some other men, and carrying only pistols, Robert captured a heavily armed ship called the *Rosamond*. He had to wade chest-high through the cold waters of the Solway Firth, which can't have improved his health. But what an exciting tale to tell his sons!

Although conscientious as always, Robert didn't let authority go to his head. Finding a poor widow selling unlicensed ale at a fair, he is said to have

demanded, 'Kate, are ye mad? Do you no' ken★ that the supervisor and I will be upon you in forty minutes?' She took the hint and was nowhere to be seen when the excisemen returned.

In addition to other goods, tea was widely smuggled. Older people had been slow to take to the new luxury of tea-drinking, believing that it could result in some nameless harm to health and well-being. The younger ones were not so slow. Some-

times the lasses emptied their chaff beds, refilled them with tea and lay there under a blanket, groaning as if in childbirth. A good exciseman needed a sense of humour!

Chapter Thirteen

DUMFRIES DAYS

Jean had to part with her 'nice wee cow' when the family moved to Dumfries. At first, they lived in a road called 'the stinking vennel'* because of the raw sewage that ran down its gutter. This was a bit of a come-down from Ellisland, for they had only a middle-floor tenement flat of three small rooms and kitchen with a tiny garden. Robert must have remembered his words to a friend:

> It's hardly in a body's pow'r,
>   To keep, at times, frae being sour,
> To see how things are shar'd.
>   *'Epistle to Davie, a Brother Poet'*

Later, the family rented a larger detached house in what's now called Burns Street. Then the smells were of animal hides curing in the tannery and they wakened to the shuffle of workmen's clogs on the cobblestoned street. But they had acquired a maid-servant again and Robert received visitors in the carpeted 'spence', or parlour.

Although not smart, Jean now wore manufac-tured shoes and fine black silk stockings. She was one of the first in Dumfries to own a dress in the new gingham cloth, made at the mill. Indeed, she would have blushed to be seen in the roughly woven skirt and bodice of twenty years before.

Most of Robert's genius was now directed to song-writing and putting new words to old tunes which Jean sang over to him. Never an accomp-lished singer himself, he praised his wife's talent when he wrote:

> I see her in the dewy flowers –
>   I see her sweet and fair.
> I hear her in the tunefu' birds –
>   I hear her charm the air.
> There's not a bonnie flower that springs
>   By fountain, shaw★ or green,
> There's not a bonnie bird that sings
>   But minds me o' my Jean.
>   *'O A' the Airts the Wind Can Blaw'*

But Jean was the first to admit her lack of learning, and for social life and mental stimulation Robert

looked elsewhere. He became increasingly interested in politics, regularly reading the newspapers which arrived several times each week. Already, they had told him of rebellion in the American colonies, but now the main stories were about Britain's war with republican France. Robert joined the Dumfries Volunteers and was kept busy (for as long as his health allowed) drilling and target-shooting as a means of home defence. Fired with patriotic enthusiasm, he tactlessly wrote to Mrs Dunlop calling the murdered King and Queen of France 'unprincipled blockheads'. As some members of Mrs Dunlop's family were staunch supporters of the French royal family, letters from her ceased abruptly!

Robert had made a mistake; something we can all do, as he once pointed out:

> Then gently scan★ your brother man,
>   Still gentler sister woman;
> Tho' they may gang a kennin wrang★
>   To step aside is human.
>   *'Address to the Unco Guid'*

But he made new friends to the end of his days. Captain Robert Riddell, who had endeared himself to Robert by setting up a library for his tenants, gave him access to a small summer house on his country estate and here the poet had privacy to write. Through this new friend, he met the witty and beautiful Maria Riddell, who offered intelligent and understanding companionship.

He became a patron of the new Dumfries Theatre and was a regular attender at performances.

Certainly he spent time drinking, as he had always done, but his poor health would never allow him to indulge too much. What could be wrong with a warming 'stoup', or tankard, to ward off the cold? Something *had* been wrong when Ann Park (who worked in the Dumfries Globe Tavern) produced Robert's baby daughter, just nine days before Jean bore his third son. But Jean's understanding in the matter was astounding, for she brought baby Betty up as her own. Laughing, she is said to have commented, 'Our Rab should have had twa wives.'

Robert was working from five in the morning until seven at night and riding 200 miles each week. Certainly, the new turnpike roads (made and repaired with the money from tolls charged) provided faster travel than the dirt roads of his younger days and he no longer had to fight his way past uncut hedges and overflowing ditches. But the winter was hard and, at times, there were drifts of snow nine metres deep. Soon, his weak heart made him ill again.

Since the stethoscope hadn't been invented, doctors knew little about heart disease. They sent poor Robert away to wade up to his armpits in the icy sea and to drink spring water from a well. 'I'll fight it out,' he had written to Gilbert, and fight he did, with wonderful courage. But the odds were against him and, at the age of thirty-seven, Robert went home to die.

Kindly seventeen-year-old Jessie Lewars, sister of another exciseman, helped Jean to nurse him, and for her he wrote a tender love-song:

> O wert thou in the cauld blast★
>   On yonder lea,★ on yonder lea,
> My plaidie to the angry airt,★
>   I'd shelter thee, I'd shelter thee.
>   *'O Wert Thou in the Cauld Blast'*

As the Dumfries Volunteers headed Robert's funeral procession to St Michael's church, Jean was giving birth to another son. What must her thoughts have been as she heard the doom-like tolling of the bells and the throb of the band? Now she was alone and largely dependent on charity to care for Betty Park and her own five sons, the eldest of whom was only nine. She lived in the same house for thirty-eight more years, longer than Robert's entire life. During that time, two of her sons died. Of the other three, Robert became a civil servant in London, while James and William both rose to the rank of colonel in the East India Service. Not bad for the sons of a poor maker of rhymes!

Chapter Fourteen

HUMANITY AND GENIUS

Robert Burns was one of the most fascinating people who ever lived. What was it, then, that made him so special? Why are there at least 180 monuments to him worldwide?

Perhaps it's because we all love a good story, especially if it makes us laugh or cry. In the transition from his humble birthplace to the imposing Dumfries Mausoleum, where he was reburied with Jean, lies a tale for thousands of pilgrims who visit them annually.

Robert's poetry has been translated into fifty languages. In Russia, over a million works of Burns sold within thirty years, whilst a Chinese edition sold 100,000 copies of its first printing.

Could it be that, after more than 200 years, he speaks to us still? Remember how he shared our dislike of getting up in the morning. But it goes much deeper than that. Here is a man who, despite the hard grind of agricultural labour, shared all our joys and sorrows, hopes and fears, *and* was able to express them in a way that's easily memorable. As he mused:

> But pleasures are like poppies spread:
>   You seize the flow'r, its bloom is shed;
> Or like the snow falls in the river,
>   A moment white – then melts for ever;
> > *'Tam o' Shanter'*

What words could be more beautiful; what experience more familiar? No wonder some of the quotations in this book are in everyday use throughout the English-speaking world.

Most widely known of all are his immortal words about friendship and parting, still sung at the end of formal gatherings. Indeed, the words ring out simultaneously throughout the length and breadth of Britain to bring in each New Year.

> Should auld acquaintance be forgot,
>   And never brought to mind?
> Should auld acquaintance be forgot,
>   And auld lang syne?★

Just watch the confusion next time this is sung! Everyone knows that hands are joined in a circle to commemorate past friendships, but *when* should the hands be crossed? The words make it clear.

The chorus follows the first verse:

> For auld lang syne, my dear,
>   For auld lang syne,
> We'll tak' a cup o' kindness★ yet
>   For auld lang syne.

Then, *and only then*, should everyone cross hands, singing:

> And there's a hand my trusty fiere★
>   And gie's a hand o' thine
> And we'll tak' a right guid-willie waught★
>   For auld lang syne.

'Auld Lang Syne'

Finally, as the chorus is repeated, the singers advance into the centre of the circle. They're making it close up, to represent continuing friendship.

Robert wanted freedom and justice for all, and one day perhaps his wish will come true:

> Then let us pray that come it may
> (As come it will for a' that)
> That man to man, the world o'er
> Shall brithers be for a' that.
> *'A Man's a Man for A' That'*

The simplicity and stirring sincerity of words like these have made Robert Burns one of the greatest poets of all time and have endeared him to the whole world.

GLOSSARY

a cup o' kindness	a friendly drink
a kennin wrang	a little bit wrong
auld lang syne	past times
bamboozle	puzzle
banes	bones
bawbees	halfpennies
braw	fine
breeks	breeches
brose	savoury porridge
but and ben	kitchen and 'good' room
carlin	old woman
cauld	cold
cauld blast	cold wind
chaff	bed of heather and brushwood
chapman	travelling salesman
chuckie stanes	large pebbles (easily thrown)
claes	clothes
claught	clawed
cockie-leekie	fowl boiled with leeks

coggies	wooden bowls
creepie	low
cutty sark	(the one in the) short shirt
dominie	schoolmaster
dram	measure (of whisky)
eldritch skreich and hollow	piercing screech and holla
enow	enough
fash	trouble
fatt'rils	ribbon-ends
fiere	companion
flail	beater
fyl'd	dirtied
gang aft agley	often go wrong
gang in stirks	start off as bullocks
gars	makes
glaikit	foolish
guid-willie waught	goodwill drink
guid-wives	farmers' wives
hashes	fellows
haud	stay
heckler	flax processor
heuk	sickle
ingle	fire
it gars me greet	it makes me weep
jouk	conceal oneself

kailyard	vegetable patch
ken	know
kist	chest
lum	chimney
mantle	covering
midden	muck-heap
mort sheets	shrouds
muckit oot	cleaned out
mutch	bonnet
plaidie	loose woollen cloak
prentice	apprentice
privy	outdoor toilet
rigs	strips for cultivation
scan	examine
Scotia's	Scotland's
shade	ghost
shaw	spinney
sic	such
skelp	smack
skelpit on thro dub and mire	scurried on through puddles and mud
sleekit	glossy-coated
slight	skill
sonsie	plumply cheerful
souter	shoemaker
steading	farmstead
swee	swinging metal pot-arm

tapmost	topmost
tapsalteerie	topsy-turvy
tatties and neeps	potatoes and turnips
to the angry airt	abandoned to the elements
vennel	lane
wad eat that want it	would like to eat but haven't food
wantons	flits
weans	children
weel	well
ye'se a' be het	you'll be all hot (i.e. roasted in hell)
yonder lea	grassland over there

INDEX OF POEMS QUOTED